Author:
Alex Woolf studied history at Essex University, England. He is the author of over 60 books for children, including *You Wouldn't Want to Live Without Fire!*, *You Wouldn't Want to Live Without Soap!*, and *The Science of Acne and Warts: The Itchy Truth About Skin.*

Artists:
Paco Sordo
Bryan Beach

Editor:
Jacqueline Ford

© The Salariya Book Company Ltd MMXVIII
No part of this publication may be reproduced in whole or in part, or stored in a retrieval system, or transmitted in any form or by any means, electronic, mechanical, photocopying, recording, or otherwise, without written permission of the publisher. For information regarding permission, write to the copyright holder.

Published in Great Britain in 2018 by
The Salariya Book Company Ltd
25 Marlborough Place, Brighton BN1 1UB

ISBN-13: 978-0-531-22768-8 (lib. bdg.) 978-0-531-23078-7 (pbk.)

All rights reserved.
Published in 2018 in the United States
by Franklin Watts
An imprint of Scholastic Inc.

A CIP catalog record for this book is available
from the Library of Congress.

Printed and bound in China.
Printed on paper from sustainable sources.
1 2 3 4 5 6 7 8 9 10 R 27 26 25 24 23 22 21 20 19 18

SCHOLASTIC, FRANKLIN WATTS, and associated logos are trademarks and/or registered trademarks of Scholastic Inc.

Scholastic Inc., 557 Broadway, New York, NY 10012

PAPER FROM
SUSTAINABLE
FORESTS

The Science of Rocks and Minerals

The Hard Truth About the Stuff Beneath Our Feet

written by
Alex Woolf

Illustrated by
Paco Sordo

Franklin Watts®
An Imprint of Scholastic Inc.

Contents

Introduction

At first sight, rocks don't seem very interesting. They're often quite dull in color, and when you kick one accidentally, it hurts! However, when you look at rocks more closely, they're actually fascinating. Almost as old as our planet, rocks are formed and shaped by heat, wind, water, and immense amounts of pressure. You can see the evidence of their long and violent history in their color, shape, and texture.

In addition to rocks, Earth is full of minerals. In fact, rocks themselves are made out of minerals. These are naturally occurring solids found in the earth. Unlike rocks, minerals have the same chemical structure (they're made of the same stuff) all the way through. Minerals include gold, copper, diamonds, quartz, and mercury. In this book we will look at how rocks and minerals are formed, how and where they can be found, and the many ways in which they are used.

Eight elements make up 98 percent of Earth's crust: oxygen, silicon, aluminum, iron, calcium, sodium, potassium, and magnesium.

Earth's Crust

Our planet is made up of layers. The outermost of these layers is the crust. If you think of Earth as an egg, the crust is its thin, hard shell. Beneath the crust is the mantle, a vast mass of hot rock. Beneath the mantle are the super-hot inner core and the outer core. Most of Earth—around 85 percent—is the mantle. The crust makes up just 0.4 percent of Earth's mass, yet it is the only part of our planet that we ever see or explore. The crust is mainly a solid mass of rocks and minerals known as bedrock. Above this is a loose layer of sand, soil, clay, and crumbled rocks.

Two Types of Crust

The crust that covers the dry parts of the world is different from the crust beneath the oceans. Continental crust is around 18 to 31 miles (30 to 50 kilometers) deep, while oceanic crust is just 3 to 6 miles (5 to 10 km) deep.

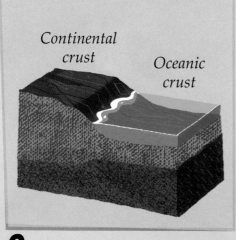

Continental crust

Oceanic crust

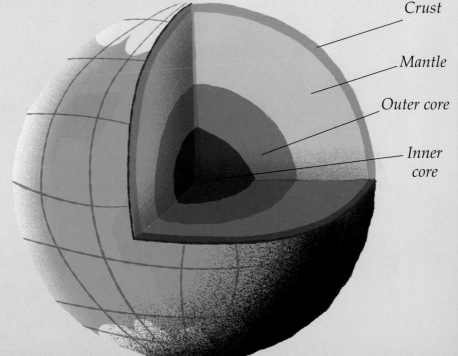

Crust

Mantle

Outer core

Inner core

Soil

The thin, topmost layer of the crust—the part we can see—is soil. Plants grow in soil, making it vital for life on Earth. Soil consists of fine rock particles, and dead plant and animal remains. Earthworms feed on these remains and increase the soil's fertility.

Not too much dear, that soil is very rich.

Outcrops

Sometimes the bedrock pokes through above the soil to the surface of Earth. This is called an outcrop. Outcrops are often found on exposed hillsides or riverbanks where the soil is worn away by wind or water. They can sometimes look quite dramatic!

A monster!

No, an outcrop.

At the weak parts of the crust, where tectonic plates meet (see right), magma (molten rock from the mantle) can rise to the surface, forming a volcano. Earthquakes are caused when tectonic plates grind against each other.

Fascinating Fact

Earth's crust and the upper mantle are broken into huge pieces called tectonic plates. These are constantly moving at a rate of a few inches per year.

Over millions of years this has caused the continents to shift thousands of miles. This process is called continental drift.

Tectonic plates

7

The Rock Cycle

Rocks are in a constant process of change from one form to another. We don't notice this "rock cycle" because it takes place very gradually over millions of years. Most rock starts as igneous rock, formed when magma cools and forms crystals. If igneous rock rises to the surface, it can change, through weathering and erosion, into sedimentary rock. If rock is deeply buried, heat and pressure will change it into metamorphic rock. Metamorphic rock can change into either igneous or sedimentary rock. The rock cycle never stops.

New rocks typically form where Earth's tectonic plates are pulling apart, causing magma to push up from the mantle. This cools down to form igneous rock.

Cooling

3

If igneous or sedimentary rock gets buried deeper in the earth, heat and pressure bake the rock. Baked rock doesn't melt, but it forms new crystals, changing it into metamorphic rock.

Cooling

Heat and pressure

Metamorphic rock

Igneous rock

Heat and pressure

Weathering and erosion

Weathering and erosion

1

Igneous rock is formed when magma (molten rock from Earth's mantle) rises to Earth's surface or closer to Earth's surface, where it cools and solidifies.

Why It Happens

When tectonic plates collide, they build mountains. The mountain-building process produces heat, and the rock becomes metamorphic. Weathering and erosion will break up the metamorphic rock, and streams will wash it away to form sediments. In this way, metamorphic rock turns into sedimentary rock.

Weathering and erosion

Compaction and cementation

2

Weathering and erosion causes igneous rock to break down into smaller and smaller pieces. Wind and water carry the small pieces into piles called sediment beds. Over time, the sediment beds get compacted and cemented to form sedimentary rock.

Sedimentary rock

q

Rocks From Fire

The word *igneous* comes from the Latin *ignis*, meaning "of fire." Igneous rock is formed when hot magma from Earth's mantle cools and solidifies. The cooling process produces crystals. If the magma cools quickly, the crystals will be small. This can happen if the magma erupts from a volcano and cools on the surface (extrusive igneous rock). Examples include obsidian and basalt. If the magma cools slowly, the crystals in the rock will be big; for example, if the magma cools underground (intrusive igneous rock). Examples include granite and gabbro.

From Lava to Rock

After magma has erupted from a volcano, it is called lava. The lava forms a thin crust that cools in 10 to 15 minutes. But the lava beneath the crust can take several months or even years to turn into rock, depending on its thickness.

Extrusive igneous rock formation

Intrusive igneous rock formation

Basalt is made from a very dark, heavy lava that can flow long distances before it cools in thin layers. Flood basalts are large stretches of land covered in solidified basalt lava. Cinder cones are cone-shaped hills created from basalt rocks blown out of a volcano.

Obsidian is a type of extrusive igneous rock that cools rapidly with very little crystal growth. As a result it is hard, smooth, and brittle, like black glass. It fractures with very sharp edges, and was used by the Aztecs to make knives and spears.

Granite

Granite is an intrusive igneous rock, usually white, pink, or gray in color. Granite contains minerals, such as quartz and feldspar, which grow crystals when the granite forms. These can easily be seen when the granite is cut and polished. Granite can be carved and shaped and is resistant to water and pollution. It has been used in construction since the time of the ancient Egyptians.

Couldn't they have built it out of something lighter?

Fascinating Fact

Granite is not found anywhere in the solar system except for Earth, and probably in low amounts on Mars.

Its volcanoes produce a strange kind of rock.

A fine blade.

The volcano should take some of the credit.

11

Rocks Under Pressure

Ripples of Time

Over time, the action of water and wind causes sand to pile up. The piles eventually get so heavy that the sand is compacted and cemented into sandstone. Ripples in the sand caused by waves and currents are sometimes preserved as patterns in the rock.

Sedimentary rock is formed when sediments (pieces of broken rock) get squished down over time by the sediments deposited above them. During this process, called compaction, water is squeezed out from between the sediments, and crystals form. The crystals produce a glue that binds the sediments together, a process called cementation. Because it forms in this way, sedimentary rock has visible layers. It may contain the fossils of animals and plants trapped there as the rock was formed. Examples of sedimentary rock include chalk, limestone, and sandstone.

One day, we'll be fossils.

Land

Material washed into sea or blown in by wind

Plant or animal dies

Layers of sediment form

Over time bottom layers turn into rock

Crack-Marked Rocks

Mudstone forms like sandstone, except the rock particles are too small to be called sand. When mud hardens, the surface sometimes cracks, and these cracks can be preserved in the rock. Occasionally, mudstone can be found with the marks of falling raindrops.

Don't worry, those cracks are pretty old!

One very rare kind of sedimentary rock comes from space. Sometimes an asteroid hits Earth so hard, it breaks up rocks and fuses them together into a new sedimentary rock.

Limestone

Some sedimentary rocks are made from the remains of living creatures. For example, limestone is formed from animal shells. When an animal with a shell dies, the living tissue decays, but the shell can help form limestone rock. Chalk is a form of limestone.

Funny to think that one day we might be used to write on a blackboard.

Okay, let's call it a draw.

Can You Believe It?

One famous fossil called "the fighting dinosaurs" was found in China in a giant sand dune that had turned to rock. Experts believe a Velociraptor and a Protoceratops were fighting when they were trapped by a collapsing sand dune.

13

Marble

The ancient Greeks called marble the "shining stone." Its beauty, softness, and waxy surface have made it a popular material for sculptors since ancient times. Marble is actually a metamorphic rock formed from the sedimentary rock limestone.

Michelangelo, why are you sculpting David?

I didn't have enough marble for Goliath.

Of the three kinds of rock that form Earth's continents, metamorphic rock is the most common.

Rocks That Change

Metamorphosis is an ancient Greek word meaning "to change form." Metamorphic rock got its name because it always starts out as a different kind of rock— sedimentary, igneous, or even as another type of metamorphic rock. The original rock is subjected to very high heat and pressure deep under Earth's surface. This can be due to contact with magma or by collisions between tectonic plates. Over time, these processes cause physical and chemical changes in the rocks. Slate and marble are both metamorphic rocks.

Pressure

Pressure

Pressure

Metamorphic rock forming

Layers of sedimentary rock

Heat and pressure

Magma

Slate

Slate is a metamorphic rock formed from the sedimentary rocks mudstone or shale. It is made up of thin, flat layers that can be split apart. Slate is often used to make roof tiles. The smooth flatness of its layers makes it an ideal base for pool tables. In the 19th century it was used for blackboards and writing slates.

Try It Yourself

You can see for yourself how heat and pressure can change things permanently. Try squeezing a piece of bread between your hands and make it into a ball. Like metamorphic rock, it has been changed and can't change back.

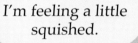

I'm feeling a little squished.

Faulty Fossils

Fossils are sometimes found in metamorphic rocks, but only if the rock was formed from a sedimentary rock that already had a fossil in it. However, the fossil is likely to be crushed, twisted, or stretched by the physical changes in the rock.

Slate is an example of a foliated metamorphic rock. These are rocks found closer to Earth's surface or produced by low pressure. They consist of parallel bands, or layers.

Minerals

Around 99 percent of minerals found in Earth's crust are made up of eight elements: oxygen, silicon, aluminum, iron, calcium, sodium, potassium, and magnesium.

Minerals are solid substances that are found naturally in the earth. They differ from rocks because they have the same chemical structure throughout. Minerals may be made of a single element (like copper) or a combination of elements (like fluorite, which is made of calcium and fluorine). We use minerals in lots of different ways. For example, the mineral quartz is used to make glass. Humans need the mineral calcium for healthy bones and teeth. Milk is a good source of calcium.

Luster

One way that scientists define minerals is by their luster—how they reflect light. They describe luster with words like glassy, dull, greasy, metallic, pearly, silky, and waxy. Opal, for example, is described as greasy, and gypsum as silky.

I would call its luster metallic.

Maybe that's because it contains metal.

You need more milk for your bones.

I can get that from milk chocolate.

16

Hardness

Another measure of minerals is their hardness—how easy it is to scratch their surface. Scientists use the Mohs' scale to measure hardness. The softest mineral, talc, is 1 on the Mohs' scale; the hardest, diamond, is 10.

Mohs' Awards

Streak

Another way that mineralogists define minerals is by their streak. This is its color in powdered form. To determine a mineral's streak, they rub it across a hard surface, such as a tile. A mineral's color is sometimes different from the color of its streak.

Mineralogists often talk about a mineral's cleavage. This means how it breaks into pieces. For example, some minerals break into small cubes, while others may break up into thin sheets.

Can You Believe It?

Call yourself a mineral?

Although we say that minerals are all solid, there is one exception: Mercury is the only mineral, and the only metal, that is liquid at normal temperatures.

Crystal shapes

Crystals form all sorts of shapes. They can have flat surfaces called facets, which can be triangular, rectangular, or square. Some crystals look like boxes with 6, 8, or even 12 sides. Others have more complex shapes.

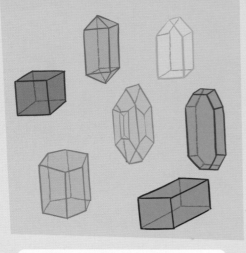

A few minerals produce liquid crystals. These are half solid, half liquid materials. They flow like a liquid yet their molecules are arranged in an ordered way, like a solid crystal. Most TV screens use liquid crystals for display.

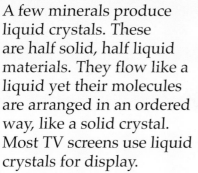

Crystals

Minerals grow crystals, which form when molten rock cools and then hardens slowly. Electrical forces cause atoms in the rock to cling to each other. As they do this they form regular, three-dimensional patterns, which become crystals. This is how valuable crystals, such as diamonds, emeralds, and rubies, are formed. Another way crystals can form is when water evaporates from a mixture. For example, salt crystals can develop as saltwater evaporates.

These rocks are boring!

Cave Crystals

Sometimes crystals form when hot underground water finds its way into cracks and holes in the rock and slowly deposits minerals. When the water cools, sparkling crystals form in the cavities. Some of the biggest crystals in the world have been found in the Cave of Crystals in Naica, Chihuahua, Mexico.

Try It Yourself

Grow your own crystals! In a beaker, stir half a cup of Epsom salts with half a cup of very hot tap water for at least a minute. Add a couple of drops of food coloring if you want a colored crystal. Put the beaker in the refrigerator. In a few hours it will be full of crystals.

According to my quartz watch, you're 0.0000002 seconds late!

Crystals Keep Time

If an electric current is passed through some crystals, such as quartz, they vibrate at a very precise frequency. Quartz crystals are used in watches and other electronic devices to keep accurate time.

Snowflakes are ice crystals that are formed in the clouds when water freezes. They always have six sides, but every one of them is unique.

19

Gemstones

Diamonds

Diamonds are crystals of carbon, and they are the hardest natural substance on Earth. They are formed under extremely high temperatures and pressures deep in the mantle, up to 118 miles (190 km) underground, then lifted closer to the surface by volcanic eruptions.

It's been on quite a journey to reach my finger.

Pure diamonds are colorless, but impurities can make them blue, yellow, orange, red, green, pink, brown, and even black.

Of all the crystals formed by minerals, the rarest and most beautiful are known as gemstones. When they are first mined, these crystals may look fairly dull. But once they are cut and polished, they display the brilliance and luster that makes them so highly valued. Gemstones are divided into two classes: precious and semiprecious. The four types of precious gemstones are diamond, ruby, sapphire, and emerald. The many semiprecious stones include amethyst, beryl, and topaz. Amethyst used to be precious, until large reserves of it were found in Brazil, reducing its rarity value.

I used to be precious—until that bunch showed up!

Sapphires and Rubies

These are both crystals of the mineral corundum. Rubies are red because they contain traces of the element chromium. Sapphires come in different colors, but the most prized ones are blue. Both stones are rare and expensive, though cheaper, artificial ones can be produced in laboratories.

I was formed in a metamorphic rock over thousands of years.

I was grown in a lab in 6 months!

Some gems aren't minerals at all. Lapis lazuli is a rock, amber is fossilized tree resin, jet is a form of coal, and pearls are made by oysters.

Emeralds

Famed for its green color, emerald is a crystal of the mineral beryl. The most valuable emeralds are judged not only on their color but also on their clarity—they must have transparency to be considered top gems. Emeralds have been mined in Egypt since around 1500 BCE. Cleopatra famously adored emeralds.

I wonder what she likes? Diamonds, sapphires, or rubies?

Why It Happens

Diamond and graphite are both crystals of carbon, yet couldn't be more different. While diamond is the hardest mineral, graphite is one of the softest. Why? Because carbon atoms bond in three dimensions in diamond, but only in two dimensions in graphite.

From copper we get two important alloys. Combined with tin, it produces bronze, a much harder metal. Copper mixed with zinc produces brass, which is highly malleable and used to make, for example, musical instruments.

Metals

Many of Earth's minerals are metals. What are metals? They are surprisingly hard to define, because it's a very broad term. In fact, over three-quarters of the elements in the periodic table are metals. They cover everything from lead (a very heavy metal) to aluminum (a very light one). Metals are usually hard and solid. Yet they include mercury, which is normally liquid, and sodium, which is soft enough to cut like cheese. Metals tend to be good conductors of electricity and heat.

Iron and Steel

Here, boy!

Iron is the most abundant element in the earth. It's a soft, gray metal and the most magnetic of the elements. Alloys of iron include steel, cast iron, and wrought iron. Steel is extremely strong, flexible, and inexpensive; and is used to build cars, ships, bridges, buildings, and tools.

What is metal?

Hard, shiny stuff.

Awesome music!

If only I had a thin sheet of metal to cover this with.

Aluminum

Aluminum is the most popular nonferrous (non-iron-based) metal, used in food packaging, drink cans, cars, aircraft, and cell phones. Despite its abundance in the earth, it couldn't be produced in mass quantities until 1886 when a practical process was invented to extract aluminum from the compound alumina.

I'm actually made of copper. The metal reacted with oxygen in the air, turning me green.

Copper

Copper was the first metal to be used by humans. The earliest tool is a copper awl (for piercing holes), dating to around 5100 BCE. Copper remains popular to this day, ranking third among metals after iron and aluminum. Because it's ductile (easily stretched into a wire) and a good conductor of electricity, copper is used in electronics and wiring.

Fascinating Fact

Iron is the sixth most abundant element in the universe. Many meteorites contain iron, and the red color of Mars is due to its iron-rich soil. Here on Earth, iron is an essential nutrient for plants and animals. It helps transport oxygen in our bodies.

I'm getting my essential iron!

The importance of rocks and metals in human history is reflected in the names we give historical eras: the Stone Age, the Bronze Age, and the Iron Age.

All the gold in Earth's crust originated from space. Scientists believe a meteor bombardment 4 billion years ago brought this gold to our planet. Superheated water bearing traces of the gold flowed through cracks within rocks. These veins of gold are mined today. Some estimate 80 percent of Earth's gold remains buried underground.

Gold

There are some metals, known as precious metals, that are valued for their rarity. These include silver and platinum, but the most cherished of all is gold. For thousands of years, gold has been a symbol of wealth, used in jewelry, coins, and works of art. Because of its cost, most of the gold we come across is not pure, but mixed with other metals. Karats are used to measure gold's pureness. Pure gold is 24 karats. For centuries, alchemists conducted experiments to try to turn base metals, such as lead, into gold. This was the origin of the modern science of chemistry.

Gold is the most ductile and malleable of all the metals. A lump of gold weighing 1 ounce (28 grams) can be stretched into a thread 5 miles (8 km) long.

You've turned lead into gold! How?

Um … I can't remember.

Panning

Some gold-bearing rocks crumble through weathering and erosion. The gold is carried away by rivers, settling where the river slows. Many people try to "pan" for this gold. They fill their pan with river water and shake. Any gold will sink to the bottom of the pan, because it's heavy.

How much is gravel worth?

The Medical Metal

Gold is regularly used for dental fillings. Injectable gold has been used to reduce pain and swelling in patients with tuberculosis. The metal is even being tested as a treatment for cancer.

Your gold medicine is wonderful, Doctor—except for the price!

Can You Believe It?

You can eat gold! Some top chefs use edible gold leaf that adds glitter to everything from cakes and pastries to olive oil. The gold isn't digested—it just passes straight through you. Only the purest gold leaf (22 to 24 karat) that is specially processed for cooking can be used for eating.

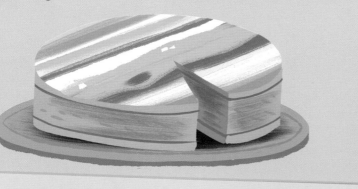

Gold is a noble metal, meaning it does not react much with anything. This means it does not degrade through exposure to air or moisture.

Mining

E arth is full of resources that we use in our everyday lives. These include many of the rocks and minerals we've looked at in this book, such as granite, limestone, marble, gold, silver, diamonds, rubies, tin, copper, and iron. Most of these resources are buried underground, and to reach them, people must dig mines. But how do they know where to mine? Geologists study rock formations and test the physical and chemical properties of soil and rocks to locate potential mineral deposits.

Shaft Mining

Shaft mines are built to obtain minerals such as iron or gold from deep underground. Shafts are dug vertically into the earth until they meet a seam. Miners then dig horizontal shafts to dig out the minerals in the seam.

I've studied the geology. There's definitely gold under here.

Open-Pit Mining

Open-pit mines, or quarries, are big holes in the earth with terraced sides from which rocks and minerals are extracted. Gravel, sand, and copper are obtained by this method.

We quarry sand here.

So it's basically a huge sandbox!

One of the earliest mines was the turquoise mine built by the ancient Egyptians at Wadi Maghareh in Sinai, more than 4,000 years ago.

Extracting Ores

Once they have been dug out of the ground, metals need to be extracted from their ores. This can involve chemical treatment (for example, with acid), electrolysis (passing an electric current through it), or heating. To obtain iron, iron oxide ore is heated in a blast furnace to remove oxygen, leaving iron behind.

Iron ore, coke, limestone

Hot waste gases

Hot waste gases

752°F (400°C)

Blast furnace

1,372°F (1,800°C)

Hot air blast

Hot air blast

Tap hole for iron

Molten iron

Can You Believe It?

The deepest mine on Earth is the Mponeng gold mine in South Africa. The mine is over 2.5 miles (4 km) deep, and the trip from the surface to the bottom takes over an hour. Geologists have drilled as deep as 7 miles (11 km) beneath Earth's surface to extract rock samples.

27

How We Use Rocks and Minerals

Making Use of Metal

During our lives, we use on average:

- 3,600 pounds (1,633 kilograms) of aluminum
- 1,278 pounds (580 kg) of copper
- 32,767 pounds (14,863 kg) of iron
- 805 pounds (365 kg) of lead
- 750 pounds (340 kg) of zinc

Some people need more metal than others.

We have been using rocks and minerals since the dawn of civilization. Rocks and stones were the very first building blocks, and they remain the most important construction material after wood. Common metals, like iron and copper and their alloys, have been used to make tools and weapons. Today, we are using rocks and minerals at an ever-increasing rate, to build machines, factories, roads, cities, and everyday objects.

Beverage cans from aluminum

Glass from quartz or silica sand

Food cans from steel

Salt from rocks

Plates from clay

Floor tiles from slate, sandstone, or marble

Pipes from copper or iron

Aggregate Is Everywhere!

One of the main building materials in our towns and cities is aggregate, or crushed stone. Sometimes this is visible as gravel; often you can't see it because it's been mixed with cement to make concrete, or with tar to create asphalt, used for roads, roofs, and parking lots.

Once, all this was forest. But someday it will be asphalt.

Hope you come back as something more interesting—like an airplane.

The metal uranium is used to create nuclear energy to give us heat, hot water, and electricity.

Recycling

Filing cabinets, computers, coat hangers, bicycles, door knockers, cutlery, and cooking pots all have metal in them. All that metal had to be extracted from ores in a process that requires lots of energy and causes pollution. That's why we should recycle metal objects when we no longer need them.

The minerals phosphate rock, potash, and lime are used in agricultural fertilizers to help grow the crops we eat. The water we drink contains minerals to make it clean.

Fascinating Fact

In every car there are over 15,000 components made from minerals.

29

Glossary

Alchemist Someone who attempted to convert base metals into gold.

Alloy A metal made by combining two or more metallic elements.

Asteroid A large rock hurtling through space, usually hundreds to thousands of feet across.

Cast iron A hard, brittle alloy of iron and carbon that can be cast in a mold.

Cementation The binding together of mineral particles.

Compaction The compressing of particles under pressure.

Compound A substance formed from two or more elements.

Conductor (of electricity) A material capable of transmitting electricity.

Core The dense, central part of a planet such as Earth.

Crust The rocky, outermost layer of a planet such as Earth.

Crystal A solid substance with a regular, geometric form.

Ductile Able to be drawn out into a thin wire.

Erosion The process of wearing something away by wind, water, or other natural forces.

Evaporation Turning from liquid into vapor.

Fossil The remains of a plant or animal preserved in rock.

Geologist An expert in the physical structure and substance of Earth.

Igneous rock Rock formed from the solidification of lava or magma.

Magma Hot, semiliquid material beneath Earth's crust.

Malleable (of a metal) Able to be hammered or pressed into shape without breaking or cracking.

Mantle The hot region of Earth's interior between the crust and the core.

Metamorphic rock Rock that has been transformed from another kind of rock by heat and pressure.

Meteorite A piece of rock that has fallen to Earth from outer space.

Mineral A naturally occurring solid made of a single substance.

Molecule A group of atoms bonded together.

Molten Describing a material that has been liquefied by heat.

Ore A naturally occurring solid material from which a metal or valuable mineral can be extracted.

Periodic table A table of all Earth's chemical elements.

Seam An underground layer of a mineral such as gold or coal.

Sedimentary rock Rock formed from sediment deposited by water or air.

Sediments Particles carried by water or wind and deposited on the surface of the land or the seabed.

Tectonic plates The giant plates that together make up Earth's crust.

Tuberculosis An infectious disease in which swellings form in the tissues, especially the lungs.

UV rays Short for "ultraviolet radiation," a component of sunlight. Too much exposure to UV rays can damage the skin.

Wrought iron A tough, malleable form of iron suitable for forging or rolling, not casting.

Index